The
Seine River

The Seine River

Carol B. Rawlins

Watts LIBRARY

Franklin Watts
A Division of Scholastic Inc.
New York • Toronto • London • Auckland • Sydney
Mexico City • New Delhi • Hong Kong
Danbury, Connecticut

Note to readers: Definitions for words in **bold** can be found in the Glossary at the back of this book.

Photographs ©: Art Resource, NY/Erich Lessing: 18, 24; Corbis-Bettmann: 5 bottom, 9 (Yann Arthus-Bertrand), 2 (Dave G. Houser), 38 (Charles & Josette Lenars), 21; Index Stock Imagery/Sandra Baker: 13; International Stock: cover (Chuck Szymanski); Photo Images /Lee Snider: 27, 31; Photo Researchers: 37 (Adam Sylvester), 36 (P. Turnley/Rapho); Photri: 8; Robert Fried Photography: 48, 49; Stock Boston: 16 (John Elk III), 22, 46 (Patrick Ward); Stone: 29 (Joe Cornish), 35 (Chad Ehlers), 5 top, 32 (Nello Giambi), 10 (Simeone Huber), 11 (Jeremy Walker); Superstock, Inc.: 44 (Private Collection), 42; The Image Works: 14, 39 (Imapress), 47 (Ray Stott); Viesti Collection, Inc.: 25 (M. Spanger/Ask Images), 40 (Joe Viesti).

Map by Bob Italiano.

The photograph on the cover shows the Seine River in Paris. The photograph opposite the title page shows a house on the Seine in Vernon, France.

Visit Franklin Watts on the Internet at:
http://publishing.grolier.com

Library of Congress Cataloging-in-Publication Data

Rawlins, Carol B.
    The Seine River / by Carol B. Rawlins
        p. cm.— (Watts library)
    Includes bibliographical references and index.
    ISBN 0-531-11853-3 (lib. bdg.)   0-531-13990-5 (pbk.)
    1. Seine River (France)—History—Juvenile literature. 2. Seine River Valley (France)—Description and travel—Juvenile literature. [1. Seine River (France)] I. Title. II. Series.
DC611.S461 R39 2001
944'.36—dc21   00-039874

Contents

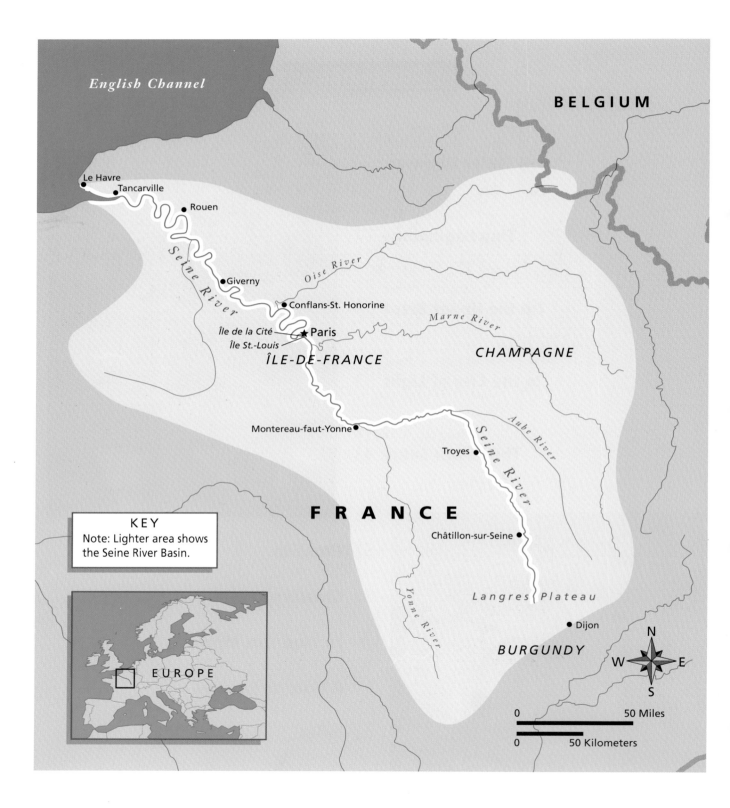

English Channel

BELGIUM

Le Havre
Tancarville
Rouen

Seine River

Giverny

Oise River

Conflans-St. Honorine

Marne River

Île de la Cité
Île St.-Louis
Paris

ÎLE-DE-FRANCE

CHAMPAGNE

Montereau-faut-Yonne

Troyes

Seine River

Aube River

FRANCE

Châtillon-sur-Seine

KEY
Note: Lighter area shows
the Seine River Basin.

Yonne River

Langres Plateau

Dijon

EUROPE

BURGUNDY

N
W   E
S

0   50 Miles

0   50 Kilometers

Chapter One

A Water Highway

The Seine River begins on the Langres Plateau, 18 miles (30 kilometers) northwest of Dijon, France. The river moves in great sweeping loops across Burgundy and Champagne, historic **provinces** known for their unique grapes and wine. The Seine flows across the Île-de-France, a rich farming region, and into Paris, the capital of France. From there, the river winds its way to the English Channel.

A barge transports goods to the city of Paris.

For centuries, the Seine has been an important route across northern France. This wide **navigable** river allowed travel, trade, and communication to flourish at a time when parts of Europe were still isolated from the outside world. Today, it carries more inland traffic than any other river in France. The Seine is the backbone of a great network of rivers and canals that carry products from oceangoing ships in the English Channel to France and neighboring nations. Cargo from oceangoing ships is unloaded at the port of Le Havre on the English Channel and transferred to **barges**. These barges deliver the products to French river ports and to connecting waterways in Belgium and Germany.

A Country of Waterways

The five major French rivers—the Seine, the Rhine, the Loire, the Garonne, and the Rhône-Saône Rivers—have linked the communities of France together for centuries. These rivers were further connected at one time by 3,300 miles (5,300 km) of canals.

The Seine is linked to the Rhine River through the Marne River, the most important of the Seine's **tributaries**. The

This photo shows where the Seine and Marne Rivers meet.

Peaks and Valleys

France's landscape includes dense forests, broad flat plains, Mediterranean beaches, and snowcapped mountain ranges. Mont Blanc, which rises 15,771 feet (4,807 meters), in the French Alps is the highest point in France and the second highest in Western Europe. The **plateau** of the Massif Central Mountains in south central France covers one-sixth of the country.

Rhine runs north between France and Germany to the North Sea, through the most populated region in Europe. The Oise River, another major Seine tributary, links the Seine River system to the waterways of Belgium.

The Seine River Basin

The Seine River Basin is known for its rich soil, fed by the waters of the Seine and its tributaries. The basin spans approximately 30,000 square miles (77,700 square kilometers)—about 15 percent of France. The Aube, Yonne, Marne, and Oise Rivers, the Seine's major tributaries, drain into the Seine River Basin.

The fertile center of the Seine River Basin is called the Île-de-France, which means the "island of France." This strip of land is called an island because the rivers that flow toward

The Seine River Basin is known for its rich farmland.

Paris, cut the region into lush river valleys. Many farms in the Île-de-France region grow wheat, barley, and corn, and raise dairy cattle. Along with the farmland, this region includes forests and the country's capital—Paris. As a result, Île-de-France is also considered the political heart of France. Called "Francia" by the Franks who once dominated the area, this was the original "France." Other regions were added later and France became the country it is today.

A Gentle Waterway

The Seine is the most navigable river in France, having few features that interfere with the movement of ships and boats. The Seine's current is so constant and slow that sometimes it almost seems to stop moving. Elevation and length of descent are two of the factors that determine the speed of a river.

The Seine rises 1,545 feet (471 meters) above sea level, which is not high as rivers go, so the river's descent to sea level is not steep. By contrast, the Colorado River in the southwestern United States descends almost 15,000 feet (4,572 m). About 30 miles (48 km) from its **source**, the Seine has already descended to 800 feet (244 m), half the distance to sea level. At Paris, 227 miles (365 km) from its source, the river is only 80 feet (24 m) above sea level.

Another feature that helps to make traveling on the Seine easier is the stability of the river channel—the land around it. The river's banks and the riverbed shift very little. The river also develops few sandbars until it reaches the port of Rouen.

After Rouen, however, where the calm waters of the Seine meet the rougher ocean water, ships must be piloted past treacherous sandbars.

Ships also have difficulty with the Seine's sweeping loops. The river turns and twists like a snake. The Seine loops back on itself so often that it actually travels only 250 miles (402 km) when measured as a straight line from its source to its mouth. Because large boats had difficulty navigating its twists and turns, thirty-nine **cuttings**, or shortcuts, have been built across the sharpest bends.

A tour boat travels on the calm waters of the Seine in Paris.

Canal Locks

Canal locks are used to keep the right amount of water in the shortcuts on the Seine. A canal lock is a stretch of water enclosed by gates at each end. It provides a means of raising or lowering vessels. When a ship enters a lock, the gate is closed behind it. The water in the lock then is raised or lowered until its level equals that of the water ahead. The ship then passes out the forward gate.

Climate of the Seine

During annual spring thaws and heavy spring rains, rivers that begin at elevations high enough to have snow and ice may send torrents of water rushing down into the lower parts of the rivers, causing their banks to overflow. Only one Seine tributary, the Yonne River, has snow and ice along its upper reaches. Today, dams and **reservoirs** on the lower Yonne control its waters before they affect the Seine.

Flooding has occurred a few times in the low-lying areas of Paris, but it is usually caused by heavy rainfall rather than a spring thaw. Precipitation is modest in the Seine Basin—25 to 30 inches (63 to 76 centimeters) per year—and rainfall is distributed evenly over the year, so flooding is not a regular problem. In 1910, however, exceptionally heavy rainfall caused the river to rise above 28 feet (8.5 m) at Paris. Serious flooding also occurred in 1993 and 1995. The average flow of the Seine at Paris is measured at 10,000 cubic feet (283 cubic meters) per second.

The **mouth** of the Seine faces another type of water problem—**tidal surges**, which are known in France as the *mascaret*. At certain times of the year, the incoming tide in the English Channel surges far up into the Seine's **estuary**—the wide mouth of the river where it meets the sea. Continued **dredging** has helped deepen the river so that the effects of the tidal surges are lessened.

Fields and hills filled with yellow blossoms can be found near the source of the Seine River.

Chapter Two

Tiny Beginnings

In a forest glade on the Langres Plateau, three tiny streams emerge from the bottom of a cliff 1,545 feet (471 m) above sea level. Farmers in this region grow mustard plants and its hills are golden with the bright-yellow mustard blossoms. These tiny streams are the **headwaters** of the Seine River. They come together in a pool that is now part of a small park owned by the City of Paris. Napoleon III, Emperor of France from 1852–1870, marked the site with a monument.

In ancient times, many people came to this pool near the source of the Seine for its healing powers.

The Little Seine (La Petite Seine), as the first segment of the great river is called, is scarcely 4 inches (10 cm) wide as it leaves the park that marks its source. Here the Seine is calm and quiet. The clear, trout-filled stream winds its way through green valleys, past villages with stone houses, and through scattered forests. Its looping course is one of the Seine's most distinctive features.

The River Goddess

Few people visit the source of the river today. Centuries ago, however, the site bustled with pilgrims who came to bathe in the sacred pools of the goddess Sequana. People worshiped Sequana as the goddess of the river and believed that she had healing powers.

In the park in 1963, **archaeologists** uncovered a statue of Sequana. She is portrayed as a young girl in Greek robes with a crown on her head. She stands in a small boat with a swan-shaped prow. The swan holds a piece of fruit in its mouth. Along with the statue, archaeologists found small metal sculptures of legs, eyes, and other body parts that people wanted Sequana to heal.

Roman temples from several periods were also unearthed at the site. Under the Roman temples, archaeologists discovered a wood and clay building. This structure was from an even earlier period, when Celtic people from the Rhine Valley in what is now Germany settled near the river.

Many of the pilgrims to Sequana's pool came from an island settlement **downriver** in what is now the heart of Paris. The island people, known as the Parisii, were boaters, fishers, and traders. *Par* is a Celtic word, meaning "boat." When the Parisii outgrew their island, they moved onto the banks of the Seine.

The Parisii boaters ruled the river until 52 B.C. Back then, people preferred to travel by river because it was safer—bandits often attacked those who traveled over land. A protective stockade surrounded the Parisii island and a market provided food and other necessities. The island people

Wandering Tribes

Countries, as we know them today, did not develop in Western Europe until the 1400s or 1500s. Before that time, tribal groups moved across the continent, con- quering local peoples as they settled a region. Later they were absorbed by other more powerful tribes, or migrated to another location.

minted their own gold coins and provided ferry service across the river.

Trading on the Seine

The Seine River has always been a busy trade route. During the Bronze Age (1800–750 B.C.) in Europe, Greeks sailed from the Mediterranean Sea into the Rhône River near Marseille, France, then up the Rhône to the Saône River. From there, they carried their cargo overland to the Seine. They traveled down the Seine to the English Channel, and then crossed the channel to Britain to get tin and copper for making **bronze**.

Other traders from what is now Germany came to the area from the east. They crossed the Seine at the Parisii village when the river was low, or were ferried across when the river was high. These travelers were on their way to Spain to trade honey, amber, and furs for metals.

Later, after Rome conquered Britain, Caesar used the Seine River to carry supplies from Rome toward Britain. Control of the Seine and the Parisii island changed several times. The **Gauls**, as the Romans called the Celtic people, joined forces with Franks from Germany. In time, the Parisii's land was renamed Paris. Trade downstream continued, but trade from the Saône River declined.

A Gaul warrior

Many beautiful homes can be found near Châtillon-sur-Seine, which means "Castle on the Seine."

Chapter Three

On the Upper River

The first town on the Seine River, *Châtillon-sur-Seine*, developed as a major trading center at the **confluence**, or meeting place, of the Seine and the Douix Rivers. Though the Douix is the larger of the two rivers, it is only 100 feet (30 m) long, about the length of a football field, and may well be the world's shortest river.

Greeks often stopped at Châtillon-sur-Seine on their journeys to Britain to get bronze, and Celtic people from southwest Germany settled near the river during the Iron Age (about 800–500 B.C.). These people left their mark on the area. A great bronze Greek vase from nearby Mount Lassois is displayed in a museum at Châtillon-sur-Seine. The vase was found, along with other treasures, in a burial mound of a young Celtic princess who died about 2,500 years ago. The huge Vase of Vix is 5 1/2 feet (2 m) tall and decorated with soldiers, chariots, serpents, and horses. Discoveries, such as this

This section of the famous Vase of Vix shows a soldier driving a chariot.

huge bronze vase, tell us how successful some of the early traders actually were and how far they traveled from home.

Past Châtillon-sur-Seine, farther down the river, the Seine widens to 150 feet (45 m) at Bar-sur-Seine, a village of old, half-timbered houses. It was here that the Seine was first dammed to use the power of the river to turn the mill wheel of an early flourmill. Today a power station stands on the same spot.

Troubled Waters

The river at Bar-sur-Seine is still fairly clean. The village fishers expect to catch fish and trust their catch will be **edible**. However, fishers downriver—farther away from the source—

People who fish in the Seine cannot always keep what they catch because of pollution.

often throw back whatever they pull in, knowing that pollution may have made the fish unfit to eat. As the Seine moves toward Paris, water released from mills, other industrial waste, and sewage empty into the river. Trout and other **native species** of fish that require large amounts of oxygen to survive have disappeared.

A new reservoir near Troyes is one solution to several of the river's problems. When the river rises, water is channeled into the reservoir through a canal and stored in the reservoir until needed. When the river is low again—in summer or periods of little rain—water from the reservoir is released into the river through another canal. The water exchange keeps the river level constant, allowing river traffic to move smoothly all year round and reducing the amount of **pollutants**.

Before the reservoir and others like it were created, the Seine often gave off a bad smell in the summertime. The odor was intensified by changes in the river's water level. In warm weather, more water evaporates from the river. And unless there is enough rainfall to make up for lost water, the level of the river goes down. Having less water in the river to dilute the polluting substances causes an increase in the concentration of harmful, bad-smelling liquids. But now water that is put in the reservoirs when the river is high can be returned to the river when the river is low, keeping offensive odors at an acceptable level. Besides helping control pollution, the Seine Reservoir and the woodlands that surround it have become a sanctuary for birds and a place that people like to visit.

Troyes

Troyes, originally a walled Roman fortress, has been an important river settlement for centuries. During the Middle Ages—from the fifth to the fifteenth century—the city became a center of religion, arts, and literature. Many beautiful churches, such as the cathedral of Saint Pierre et Saint Paul, were built during this time. In the twelfth and thirteenth centuries, medieval knights would stop in Troyes on their way to the **crusades**, which were Christian expeditions from Europe to gain control over holy places, such as Jerusalem. Troyes was

In late 1200s, workers built the church of Saint Urbain.

Canal of the Upper Seine

In 1847, workers completed a 30-mile (48-km) straight canal from Troyes to the confluence of the Seine and Aube Rivers after forty years of digging. For the first time, barges from the English Channel could travel up the Seine into the Aube to reach Troyes by canal. Today, this canal is paved over and used as a roadway.

also the principal city of the counts of Champagne, the most powerful noblemen in France. These noblemen built a complex canal system between the branches of the Seine near Troyes.

Troyes, in the Middle Ages, was one of the most colorful cities in France, known for its great trade fairs and jousting tournaments. The city was also known for its **textiles**. At the fairs, textiles and other goods from all over Europe were bought and sold.

The city has remained an important textile center. Half the children's clothes in France are made here, as well as popular adult clothing that is sold abroad. Mills, too—sawmills, flourmills, and mustard mills—are numerous. Old churches and medieval houses still line the narrow streets of the city.

Medieval Times

In medieval France, the king gave some of his land to nobles in exchange for their loyalty, military backing, and money. Many local nobles became more powerful than the king. The people who worked the land traded their labor to the nobles in exchange for food and protection. This system of exchange was called feudalism.

Approaching Paris

Upstream from Paris, the Seine meets the Aube River, one of its tributaries. The Aube is twice as wide and its waters greenish-white—the white comes from the chalk fields it crosses. *Aube* is a Latin word meaning "white."

The Seine bears west around the Île-de-France and is joined at Montereau by the Yonne River from the southeast. Thick, green, and much larger than the Seine, the Yonne travels side by side with the Seine before the two rivers merge. Montereau is a growing town with a busy port. Barges filled with cargo move up and down the river. Local industries make bricks, process sugar, and produce farm machines.

Boats line the banks of the Yonne River, a tributary of the Seine.

Reindeer Crossing

Near the power plant in 1964, archaeologists discovered the remains of a prehistoric camp. Prehistoric hunters lay in wait here for herds of reindeer to cross the river each year.

Along with factories, many of France's sources of electricity can be found beside the Seine, including the largest electric power plant in France. This fully automated plant produces electricity for the European electricity **grid**. Large amounts of cooling water are required to carry away the heat released in that process. Water from the Seine is used to do the cooling and is then returned to the river.

France also uses nuclear power for energy. More than 75 percent of the electricity produced in France comes from nuclear-powered plants. The Loire River is a source of cooling water for a chain of nuclear-powered plants. Some scientists believe that nuclear waste from the Loire is polluting the Seine. The two rivers are linked by canals.

Saint-Mammès, at the meeting of the Seine and Loing rivers, is an important port where many ships stop to refuel. The waterfront is lined with freight-hauling barges, and the river is stained with oil. As the Seine approaches Paris, large farms and lines of poplar trees alternate with industrialized towns.

The gardens and forest of the great **chateau** of Fontainebleau stretch toward the river. This palace was the favorite hunting lodge of French kings for eight hundred years. The river passes Melun and Corbeil, where the most important grain mills in France are located.

As the Seine enters Paris, the Marne River—the Seine's greatest tributary—comes in from the northeast. The Marne links the Seine River system and the Rhine River system. The

Rhine flows northward between France and Germany to the North Sea. The Rhine is the busiest waterway in Europe and passes through the most heavily populated region in Europe. France and Germany are key members of the European Union (EU) and are each other's best trading partners.

The Seine becomes crowded in the port of Saint-Mammès.

Pont Alexandre III, one of the many bridges in Paris, lights the Seine at night.

Chapter Four

In the City of Light

Entering Paris, the Seine makes a great 8-mile (13-km) loop through the heart of the city. Paris is one of the few capital cities in the world that can be visited by river. Parisians love to watch the city lights reflected in the river at night. French people and tourists stroll along the *quays*, or riverbanks. Riverfront property in Paris is among the most expensive real estate in the world. Some Parisians spend their entire lives on the Seine, bringing up their children on barges and houseboats. Some people keep chickens in the holds of their houseboats.

Even the motto of Paris is related to the river: *Fluctuat nec Mergitur* (Sail but Do Not Sink). Streets in Paris are numbered according to whether they run parallel to the river or at right angles to it. Many of the city's most famous buildings and monuments lie along the river and can be reached by *bateaubus* (water bus). Several *ponts* (bridges) over the Seine are memorials to famous people and are decorated for special events. The United Nations Educational, Scientific and Cultural Organization (UNESCO) made the Seine River quays of Paris a World Heritage Site in 1991. UNESCO encourages and provides support to help countries preserve their cultural and natural heritage.

Life on the River

Into the 1600s, large numbers of people lived on the banks of the Seine. Later, the riverbanks were raised because the river often overflowed. Parisians bathed and washed their clothes in the slow-moving river. They used it as a dump for sewage and waste, and watered their horses in the river.

The butchering and leather-making industry added waste and odors to the river too. And floating fish markets kept their catch in boats with holes in the hull. The polluted water made disease a constant concern. When the river was low, people were banned from doing their laundry near *Île de la Cité* (City Island), the home of the Parisii.

Islands of Paris

Île St. Louis (St. Louis Island) and Île de la Cité are the two main islands in the Seine River. Hotels and the Church of St. Louis-on-the-Island now dominate Île St. Louis. Until 1614, the island was only pastureland where washerwomen came to dry their laundry and gentlemen came to fight duels. Île St. Louis connects to Île de la Cité by a footbridge.

Île de la Cité is best known for the enormous Cathedral of Notre Dame—the haunt of Quasimodo in Victor Hugo's novel, *The Hunchback of Notre Dame* (1831). This church receives about 11 million visitors a year. The island also houses government buildings, such as the Palais de Justice. In the fourteenth century, the Palais de Justice added a prison where

People come from around the world to admire the Cathedral of Notre Dame.

A smaller version of the Statue of Liberty sits on an island near the Eiffel Tower.

many famous prisoners stayed before they were executed, such as Queen Marie Antoinette, the wife of Henry XVI. The prison still holds inmates today.

A smaller model of the Statue of Liberty that France gave the United States stands on the long narrow *Île aux Cygnes* (Island of the Swans). Frédéric-Auguste Bartholdi, a French sculptor, designed the statue and Gustave Eiffel developed the iron framework needed to support it. Originally, France hoped to give the statue to the United States on July 4, 1876, to celebrate the hundredth anniversary of U.S. independence. Because of delays, the people of France gave the finished statue to a representative of the United States in Paris in 1884. It was erected and dedicated in New York in 1886.

Crossing the Seine

Thirty-six bridges span the river in Paris, each about 1,312 feet (400 m) in length. Many are beautiful works of art. The recently built Alexandre III Bridge, copied from a bridge in St. Petersburg, Russia, is decorated with stone lions, statues with gold trim, nymphs, and lamps.

Pont Neuf (New Bridge), at the end of Île de la Cité, is nearly four hundred years old. Pont Neuf was the first bridge in Paris with no houses on it. At one time, houses, mills, and arches of bridges extended into the river, narrowing the Seine by 131 feet (40 m). For centuries, much of life in Paris centered around the Pont Neuf. The bridge housed a fair where acrobats and singers performed.

Passing through narrow arches holding up Pont Neuf and other bridges was so difficult that special boaters were needed. These boaters were called "bridge swallowers" and guided boats under the bridges using special poles and ropes. Eventually, the city removed the structures standing in the river and demolished the shops on the bridges.

A boat takes visitors for a closer look at the Pont Neuf, one of the oldest bridges in Paris.

Making a Modern City

In the mid-1800s, Napoleon III and Baron Georges Haussmann, the chief city planner, rebuilt Paris. They tore down ancient walls and opened up the river area. They moved ports to the edge of town and diverted heavy barges into canals behind the city. They planted trees along the quays and cleared out old, run-down apartment buildings, or tenements, such as those on the Île de la Cité. People came from around the world to see the new Paris.

Pollution Problems

Factories and petroleum refineries, along with the city's inadequate sewer system, continue to pollute the Seine, disturbing the natural balance of marine life. During a single week in 1992, half the fish in Paris died because of an oily film on the river that cut the level of oxygen in the water. Local officials pumped billions of bubbles of oxygen into the river to prevent further deaths.

Officials say the Seine is less polluted today. Half the drinking water used in Paris is pumped from the Seine and the Marne Rivers and treated in water-treatment plants before distribution. The cloudy appearance of the water is caused by suspended mineral particles. The rest of the water consumed in Paris comes from springs.

Efforts have been made to re-create conditions that can sustain life in the polluted river. Twenty species of fish have

Pollution in the Seine has damaged the marine life in the water.

been introduced to the river, including the dace, which tolerates poor quality water better than most species. Aquatic plants are growing again in pockets in the riverbanks and on the riverbed.

Environmentalists are not satisfied though. Scientists have found fifty-seven varieties of pollution in the river. The Seine has a hundred times more bacteria than the European Union's standard for safe swimming. In spite of this, competitors in river tournaments still continue the tradition of throwing one another into the river.

The Port of Paris

Paris is the leading river port in France, and, at one time, the Seine was the city's main supply route. Meat, coal, fruit, wood, and goods of all kinds traveled to Paris by river. Today, barges loaded with grain, sand, and gravel share the river with sightseeing boats, ducks, pleasure craft, and police and fire boats, as well as foreign ships.

Modern-day Paris is closed to such river traffic at night. After dark, the river and the riverbanks belong to Parisians and tourists. Barge operators, yacht captains, and other

A barge waits for the gates to open to deliver its cargo.

business people wanting to enter Paris by river must wait for the city gates to open at 7:00 A.M.

Famous Places by the Seine

The banks of the Seine are lined with famous buildings and parks. The Louvre Museum, once the City Hall, is the world's largest art museum. It houses an art collection, including the *Mona Lisa*, *Venus de Milo*, and paintings by Rembrandt. In the 1600s and 1700s, barges delivered corn, hay, wood, vegetables, and meat for the court to St. Nicolas Port, near the Louvre.

The Louvre Museum holds many of the world's greatest works of art.

The French Revolution

The French Revolution, which began in 1789, had many causes, one of which was the oppression of the common people. France was ruled by two groups of privileged people who lived lavishly and spent extravagantly—the nobility and the church. The public treasury was bankrupt. The representatives of the Third Estate (the common people) declared themselves the National Assembly and abolished all privileges. During the Reign of Terror that followed, many people were guillotined. Eventually, Napoleon Bonaparte, a young French general, rose to power. Revolution against monarchs, nobles, and clergy spread throughout Europe. When the dust settled, the medieval power structure of France was gone forever.

Beyond the Louvre lie the Gardens of the Tuileries, all that remains of a great palace built in 1564. The Tuileries Gardens were the first large park on the Seine. At one time, a swimming pool floated in the river nearby—floating swimming pools were fashionable from the 1700s onward. In 1792, an angry crowd stormed the Tuileries Palace and arrested Queen Marie Antoinette. The queen was later **guillotined**. Her husband, King Louis XVI, was tried and executed for treason.

At several points on the river, tourists can board passenger boats or join tours through the sewers of Paris. The sewers were made famous by Victor Hugo's fictional work, *Les Miserables* (1862). The Eiffel Tower, perhaps the most famous landmark in France, is on the left bank of the Seine. **Towpaths** on the right bank are reminders of a time when men and horses on land hauled boats upriver with towropes.

Along with barges carrying heavy cargoes, you can find people visiting the Lower Seine to enjoy sailing on its waters.

Chapter Five

The Lower Seine

The stretch of river below Paris is called the Basse-Seine, or Lower Seine. The Lower Seine bustles with barges—some as large as 100 feet (30 m) long. Many of the vessels carry heavy petroleum products and building materials. Barges often refuel and pick up cargo at the barge depot of Conflans-St. Honorine. There, the Oise and Seine rivers meet, 40 miles (64 km) south of Paris. Ships can then take the Oise River to reach ports in Belgium.

Giverny

One riverside community has been featured in the paintings of Claude Monet. Monet lived in the village of Giverny at the confluence, or meeting, of the Epte and Seine Rivers and is known as one of the foremost figures in a late nineteenth-century style of painting called **Impressionism**.

Fascinated with the way sunlight reflects on water, Monet diverted water from the Seine to create a water garden with a Japanese bridge behind his house. He painted forty-eight impressions of water lilies and the bridge at different hours and seasons and produced eighteen paintings of the Seine. Other impressionist artists, such as Pierre-Auguste Renoir and Alfred Sisley, also found inspiration in the Seine River.

Many of the barge operators live on their barges in Conflans-St. Honorine after they retire. The bargees, as they are called, even celebrate weddings and attend funerals on a floating church, Saint Nicholas Chapel. Saint Nicholas is the patron saint of river people. Below Conflans, the river flows past farms growing produce for people of Paris. Cattle graze on the river banks. Many Parisians visit this area in the summer to sail on the Seine and to fish in its waters.

Normandy

At Giverny, the Seine departs the Île-de-France and enters Normandy, a historic province of France. The province was named for the Norsemen or Normans, Scandinavian Vikings who repeatedly raided northern France by sailing up the Seine River. The Norsemen murdered and looted, interfered with commerce and travel on the river, and burned the ports of Rouen and Paris. In 911, King Charles III of France made a deal with a Norse leader named Rollo. The king made Rollo the duke of Normandy and gave him control over the region, in exchange for stopping his attacks.

William II, a later duke of Normandy, crossed the English Channel and invaded England in 1066. After defeating the English, William became the king of England, and Normandy then became an English territory. France regained Normandy permanently from England in 1450, at the end of the Hundred Years War (1337–1453).

On June 6, 1944, Normandy played a historic role in World War II. Allied forces—more than 175,000 British, Canadian, and U.S. troops—landed on five beaches on the coast of Normandy. Allied troops easily took control of four

Castle of Terror

The ruins of an ancient castle sit high on a tall white cliff above the Seine River at Les Andelys. Chateau Gaillard was constructed in the 1190s by Richard the Lionheart, king of England. Moats were built to help to make it a castle that was almost impossible to capture. Ownership of the castle went back and forth between England and France until 1449 when France captured it permanently.

Chateau Gaillard has a bloody history. One king of France locked up his wife there and then had her murdered when she refused to give him a divorce. Later, bandits from the castle captured travelers on the Seine and tortured them for money. King Henry IV finally had the castle pulled down.

beaches, but fought fiercely with the Germans to gain the remaining one. From the air, Allied planes bombed some of the bridges on the Seine to stop the Germans from sending more troops into the region. This important battle led to the defeat of Nazi Germany in World War II (1939–1945).

Today, more than three million people live in Normandy. Visitors come to the region to enjoy its beautiful beaches on the coast. In the countryside, many people raise dairy cows, tend apple orchards, and grow grain. Castles, abbeys, and villages with thatched-roof houses line the banks of the Seine.

Omaha Beach is one of the five beaches on the coast of Normandy where the allies landed in 1944.

Ports of the Lower Seine

Many people visit Rouen to see some of its historic buildings.

Rouen, a historic city and major seaport, lies 75 miles (120 km) from Paris, halfway between the city and the sea. Rouen began first as a Roman camp and later became the capital of Normandy. Today, the wharves and quays at Rouen are usually crowded with ships and tankers unloading oil and taking on cattle, timber, or wine.

Over the years, Rouen has become a center for industry. Factories here make clothing, mechanical equipment, cars, and airplane parts. Much of the newsprint used by France's newspapers is made in Rouen.

Further down the Seine, Le Havre is the busiest Atlantic Ocean port in France, which stands on the right bank of the Seine estuary. Unfortunately, all of this ship traffic has had a negative effect on the area's environment. The Seine estuary is

A ship approaches the port of Le Havre.

so polluted with oil and chemicals that animal life can no longer flourish here.

Le Havre was built in the late sixteenth century to replace the port of Honfleur, which is located on the left bank. During the Middle Ages, Honfleur served as a port for the Seine Valley. The French explorer Samuel de Champlain sailed from Honfleur in 1608 to travel to North America to found Quebec, which is now part of Canada. While the bigger ships now go to Le Havre, many people visit the old harbor at Honfleur to enjoy its beauty.

Timeline

1000 B.C.	Celtic people form major settlements in France.
58–51 B.C.	France conquered by Romans under Julius Caesar; the region is called Gaul.
A.D. 52	The Parisii lose control of the Seine to Romans who use river as route to Britain.
A.D. 486	Germanic invaders, including the Franks, defeat last Roman governor.
A.D. 987	End of Franks rule over Gaul (France); feudal lords assume power.
1066	William, Duke of Normandy, invades England, becomes King of England.
1150	Great fairs at Troyes flourish.
1337–1453	The English are evicted from French soil during the Hundred Years War; Normandy is restored to France.
1431	Joan of Arc is burned at stake for treason.
1580s	Port of Le Havre replaces Port of Honfleur.
1643–1715	Under Louis XIV, France becomes greatest power in Europe.
1789	The French Revolution begins.
1793	Queen Marie Antoinette and King Louis XVI are executed.
1804	Napoleon I makes himself emperor.
1852–70	Napoleon III, Emperor of France, rebuilds Paris; places monument at source of Seine River.
1886	France gives United States the Statue of Liberty and places miniature version on Île aux Sygnes.
1872	Claude Monet's style of painting dubbed "Impressionism" influences later painters.

Continued on next page

Timeline (Continued)

1910	The waters of the Seine overflow and the city of Paris floods because of exceptionally heavy rainfall.
1914–18	France leads resistance against Germany in World War I.
1940	Germany defeats France in World War II.
1944	Allies invade Normandy on June 6; by end of year, France and Belgium are liberated.
1955	France forms the European Economic Community (EEC) with five other countries—Belgium, Germany, Italy, Luxembourg, and the Netherlands.
1963	Archaeologists uncover Roman and Celtic temples and artifacts at source of the Seine.
1964	Archaeologists discover prehistoric camp in an area where hunters waited for reindeer to cross the Seine.
1973	Denmark, Ireland, and the United Kingdom join the European Community (EC).
1981	Greece joins the European Community.
1986	Spain and Portugal join the European Community.
1991	The United Nations Educational, Scientific and Cultural Organization names the quays of Paris as a World Heritage Site.
1992	Half the fish in the Seine in Paris die because of pollution. The European Community becomes the European Union in November.
1993	The Seine floods Paris.
1995	Austria, Finland, and Sweden join the European Union; the Seine floods Paris again.
1999	The euro becomes currency for electronic transfers and accounting purposes in much of Western Europe.

Glossary

archaeologist—a specialist who scientifically studies the remains of the culture of a people

barge—a flat-bottomed boat used chiefly for the transport of goods on inland waterways; usually propelled by towing

bronze—a yellowish brown mixture of copper and tin, with other metals such as zinc, lead, and silver added

chateau—a castle, country house, or mansion

confluence—where two streams (or rivers) meet

crusades—wars undertaken by European Christians between the eleventh and thirteenth centuries to recover the Holy Land from the Muslims

cutting—a channel cut to bypass a difficult section of a river and make navigation easier

downriver—moving toward the mouth of a river

dredging—making a waterway deeper by use of a dredging machine

edible—safe to eat

environmentalist—a person concerned about human ecology

estuary—the widening channel of a river where it nears the sea

Gauls—the name given to the Celts by the Romans; the ancient Latin name for the people who lived south and west of the Rhine River, west of the Alps, and north of the Pyrenees.

grid—a network of power lines for the distribution of electricity

guillotined—a method of execution in which a person's head is cut off

headwaters—source of a stream or river

Impressionism—the name given a group of nineteenth-century artists who were fascinated by the effect of light and color.

mouth—the place where a stream enters a larger body of water

native species—a group of animals or plants with similar characteristics that originate in a particular place

navigable—deep enough and wide enough to afford passage to ships

plateau—flat land raised sharply above adjacent land

pollutant—a substance that pollutes

province—a historic region of France, such as Champagne, Burgundy, and Normandy, that was once ruled by a duke or count

reservoir—a human-made lake for storing water

source—point of origin; where a river begins

textile—woven or knit cloth

tidal surge—a tidal flood which rushes with great violence into the estuaries of some rivers at certain times of the year

towpath—a path alongside a canal or river, used by people or animals for towing boats or barges

tributary—a contributing stream or river that empties into another stream or river

To Find Out More

Books

Bjork, Christina. *Linnea in Monet's Garden*. Stockholm: R & S Books, 1987.

Dickens, Charles. *A Tale of Two Cities*. New York: Barnes and Noble Books, 1994.

Gilbert, Adrian. *Revolution! The French Revolution*. New York: Thomson Learning, 1995.

Hugo, Victor. *Hunchback of Notre Dame*. New York: Random House, Inc., 1995.

Lasby, Kathryn. *Marie Antoinette: Princess of Versaille: Austria-France, 1769*. New York: Scholastic, Inc., 2000.

Nardo, Don. *France*. Danbury, CT: Children's Press, 2000.

Organizations and Online Sites

The Eiffel Tower
http://www.tour-eiffel.fr/indexuk.html
The official website for this famous structure by the Seine offers a history of the tower and a virtual tour.

European Union
http://www.europa.eu.int/
Learn more about the European Union, the euro currency, and the fifteen member countries.

Federation of Alliances Françaises (USA), Inc.
2819 Ordway Street NW
Washington, DC 20008
http://www.afusa.org/
This non-profit cultural and educational organization is dedicated to promoting French language and culture.

French Embassy
4101 Reservoir Rd., N.W.
Washington, DC 20007
http://www.info-france-usa.org
Learn about French history, geography, and culture from the embassy's website.

The French Tourism Office

http://www.francetourism.com

Run by the official French government tourist office, this website offers a wealth of information for anyone planning a trip down the Seine or wanting to learn more about France.

The Louvre Museum

http://www.louvre.fr

Visit one of the world's most famous art museums online.

United Nations Educational, Scientific, and Cultural Organization

http://www.unesco.org/whc/nwhc/pages/home/pages/homepage.htm

From this online site, you can learn more about UNESCO's World Heritage Sites, such as the banks of the Seine in Paris.

A Note on Sources

I always start at the public library whenever I do research. First, I turn to good encyclopedias to get an overview of the topic. Articles on France gave me more detail than I could use, while articles about the Seine River left me wanting more. I found the physical features and flow patterns of the river, but not answers to my favorite questions, "what does it look like?" and "So what?" "So what?" means "why is it important that that happened?" I turned to books and found *The Secret Life of the Seine* by Mort Rosenblum and *The Seine* by Anthony Glyn especially helpful by providing a bird's eye view of life along the river. I am fortunate to have walked the quays along the Seine River myself, as a tourist.

For more detail on the river within Paris, I used two of my favorite guide books—Fodor's *Exploring Paris* and the beautiful *Knopf Guide to Paris*, which includes a fascinating historic map of Paris, as well as a map of the modern river.

The July 1989 issue of *National Geographic Magazine*, devoted to the history of France, has colorful illustrated chapters on the French Revolution. CD-ROMs of all the maps ever published by *National Geographic* showed the Seine River in great detail. CD-ROMs of *Encyclopaedia Britannica, Inc.* include a detailed map of the Seine, Rhine, and Rhône river basins, and the major canals of France.

For flavor, I read Victor Hugo's novel, *The Hunchback of Notre Dame*, and Albert Bigelow Paine's book on Joan of Arc, *The Girl in White Armor*.

—Carol B. Rawlins

Index

Numbers in *italics* indicate illustrations.

About the Author

Carol Blashfield Rawlins has deep Midwestern roots. Born in Wisconsin, she attended public schools in Illinois, graduated from Ohio Wesleyan University, and then returned to Illinois to teach high school English, history, and social studies. Later she moved to Topeka, Kansas, where she raised a daughter and son, attended graduate school at the University of Kansas, and worked for the State of Kansas.

A Californian for more than a decade, Carol and her husband enjoy following rivers from beginning to end, documenting what they see along the way. Today, they live in Santee, near San Diego. Ms. Rawlins is also the author of *The Orinoco River* and *The Colorado River* for Franklin Watts.